Civil Society, Changing Contemporary Politics with the return of multi-party politics in the Third World & Religion: An Introduction

TERRY R. LYNCH

DEDICATION

All my love
Agnes Retno Utami

CONTENTS

FORWARD

This essay seeks value from Civil Society in terms of changes in contemporary politics from its ancient origins, Tocqueville perceptions, Gramsci third force interpretations for emancipation of the disempowered and its global expansion and interpretation.

Assessing how these are achieved and looks at various critiques of the concept to offer a balanced argument. Looking at the studies of analysts such as Putnam it assesses its usefulness and highlights attitudes within society.

Revealing attitudes from society towards their democratic structures and how voting turnout, declining political membership and increasing pressure groups have seen a different approach from society towards democratic institutions.

The role of religion within this framework and a selection of key thinkers on the matter of how this civil society and religion fit and act together.

.

1 WHAT IS CIVIL SOCIETY AND WHAT CAN THE CONCEPT OFFER FROM THE STANDPOINT OF UNDERSTANDING CHANGE IN CONTEMPORARY POLITICS?

Civil Society tends to be an overused and somewhat obscured concept. The concept causes much confusion and gets somewhat lost in translation, in contemporary terms; the concept is becoming overused to the point of becoming a catchy marketing slogan.

This essay will address this problem and seek some value leading to an understanding of change in contemporary   politics.
How civil *is* society and does this concept change in description as modern society advances, as perceptions weave in and out of society does some degree of civility escape? Is there some continuity within the concept?

Change is very evident in the history of the concept, in the days of Aristotle it was considered indistinguishable from the state of direct democracy where everything was built round the state but as democracies developed, did Civil   Society   follow?

It is clear that from 1750-1850 that Civil Society evolved and became separated from the notion of the state and indeed a bulwark against an increasing state influence. It became a defence against the state, a means of controlling its excesses.

Is Civil Society a response to the perceived crisis in the ruling social order, politics or economics? At the time of the French and American revolutions, great change took place in Civil Society, this change meant replacement of a community of neighbours to a community of strangers.

The idea of Civil Society as a bulwark against the state first became present in the studies of Alexis de Tocqueville as he took America as a model for democratisation in France.

He identified vast organisations and associations which created a vibrant and dynamic community life beyond the reaches of the state; was this created through the fear of a growing state in civil life? This would support the idea of Civil Society being reactionary to state directives.

At the end of his investigation he deemed the United States "the most democratic country on the face of the earth"[1], so it enhances democracy, allows freedom of association, expression and preference?

This became known as associative life and became important because it created social harmony and trust, kept the state at bay and protected individual liberties. If this concept was to disintegrate there would be nothing to stop the state interfering into certain aspects of civilian life.

In contemporary analysis civil society can be used to measure membership to political parties and turnout to general elections highlights political participation, from this some useful and somewhat alarming statistics have emerged that offer us a greater understanding of our

---

[1] Tocqueville de, Alexis, *Democracy in America*. Frohnen, Bruce (ed.), (Washington DC: Regnery Publishing, 2002) p473

democracy.

To analyse change within the concept, it must be understood from its historical context to appreciate its contemporary form. One form of argument used extensively by Marxists and non-Marxists alike is the perception that changes in Western European nations is related to economic development combined with both an expansion and democratisation of their structure.[2]

Mark Bevir (f.1) argues that centralisation and new functions strengthened the state in relation to Civil Society. For example, the British model included reform of key parts of the state and a new strategy for economic development and new welfare initiatives (accepting more responsibility for citizens).

This wave of democratisation saw the emancipation of the working classes in 1867, 1884 and 1918[3] and their entrance into the exclusive club of Civil Society. Now with equal humane and social rights through the welfare state working men could join what Marx called *bürgerliche Gesellschaft* or "Bourgeois society"[4].

After 1945, new political and social rights were granted to citizens and through a global conflict society shared an experience that affected all. This reinforced the

---

[2] Trentmann, Frank (ed.) Paradoxes of civil society: new perspectives on modern German and British history. (Berghahn Books, 2000) p332-351.

[3] Garrad, John. Democratisation in Britain: Elites, civil society and reform since 1800 (Hampshire: Palgrave, 2002) p152-182.

[4] Poggi, Gianfranco. *Images of Society: essays on the sociological theories of Tocqueville, Marx and Durkheim* (London: Oxford University Press, 1972), p122.

community of strangers and together with reforms in economic and legislative spheres in most Western states Civil Society was somewhat strengthened.

From this, it is considerable to argue that Civil Society is now a global concept; that of a vast, interconnected and multi-layered social space[5] made up of non-governmental organisations (NGOs), civic and business initiatives, social movements, etcetera.

This is evident even in international organisations such as the United Nations (UN) whereby Kofi Annan, Secretary General stated "The United Nations once only dealt with governments...peace and prosperity cannot be achieved without partnerships involving governments, international organizations, business and civil society".[6]

John Keene presents the view that this global society is motivated by "turbo-capitalism"[7] with the aim of civilizing uncivil capitalism.

If we are to take the associative interpretation, as raised by Tocqueville, there should be impetus for a new consensus that a healthy and vibrant associative life is a key to achieving *good governance*.

The Gramsci interpretation reveals a "third force"[8] between the state and the market with a realm of potential emancipation for the disempowered.

With increased globalisation and reconciliation of the world economy it can be argued as by Andrew Linklater, that a new idealistic world political community has become

---

[5] Global Civil Society?, Keane, John, (Cambridge: Cambridge University Press, 2003) p9, 20.
[6] "Civil Society & the UN", http://www.un.org/issues/civilsociety/
[7] Global Civil Society?, Keane, John, Op. cit. p65-74.
[8] For further argument on how the welfare state, as a third force, can achieve emancipation for the disempowered read: *Power Resource Management and the welfare state* (London: University of Toronto Press, 1998) p142.

Civil Society, Changing Contemporary Politics with the return of
multi-party politics in the Third World & Religion: An
Introduction

possible[9].   However, this is a complex issue and
globalisation has different experiences within different
communities.

Therefore it is dangerous to suggest that Civil Society
is all embracing, but through international organisations
such as Fair Trade, Red Cross and others the issue of
exploitation through extended use of the media is finding
compassion within this community.

It would appear that Civil Society is disintegrating as
people are increasingly becoming disconnected from
family, friends, neighbours and our democratic structures.
Robert D. Putnam conducted an analysis of the concept
concentrating on group activities and found that we are
increasingly *bowling alone*, as bowling numbers in America
were the highest (at the time of publication) but league
numbers   were   down.

In this respect, the concept Civil Society is evidently
useful as Putnam conducted an interview of five hundred
thousand to conclude that the American people were less
politically active and more introvert highlighting an
attitude from society towards contemporary issues.

However, Putnam suggests that society can civilly
reinvent itself, proposing that the concept is indeed
flexible and can change in response to events in
contemporary   politics.   [10]
Tocqueville' proclamation of America being the most
democratic has to be now questioned as the very fabric
that kept the democratic structure underpinned and state
separate from civil life is now merging and threatening the
very   fabric   of   representative   democracy.

---

[9] The Transformation of Political Community, Linklater,
Andrew, (Cambridge: Polity Press, 1998).

[10] http://www.bowlingalone.com (cited 20/11/2005)

If this is the case then the very bulwark against the state that prevents such intrusions into aspects of social life will eventually become redundant and threaten the very principles of Liberal Democracies, however society can reinvent itself to respond to such dire times.

In analytical terms political parties help to identify preferences, these are reflected in civil Society through membership, however as they evolved they have become agents of the state, rather than representatives of the people and therefore resulted in a reduction of participation as people felt there interests were not being served.

If Civil Society is to be seen as a means of emancipation and this is to be achieved through the medium of democracy then an expansion of this society is required with a decreasing state, however the concern (in contemporary perception) is that the opposite is happening.

Was this decrease (in part) due to a realisation that society is becoming a victim of the "tyranny of the majority"[11] losing faith in Liberal Democracy as the disempowered electorate turn towards Authoritarianism.

Antonio Gramsci uses the Bolshevik Revolution and the concept of Civil Society to analyse why the revolution succeeded in Russia but had failed elsewhere? This is where change is most prevalent as old attitudes were supplanted and the hegemony of the ruling political elite maintained through Civil Society. However, this could only be gained by the offering an alternative again through such means.

In representative democracies voting is the key to the very nature of the political system, however, as Civil Society decreases less people are turning out to cast their votes. This is somewhat alarming as representatives are

---

[11] Democracy in America, Tocqueville, Alexis D., Op cit. p205-214.

gaining office with less than half the support of the constituency who could be bothered to turnout.

However, this argument requires an analysis of the electoral system; its advantages and disadvantages. As Mark N. Franklin claims with conviction that it has more to do with the character of elections, not of society and "commentators, who see in falling turnout a reflection on the civic-mindedness of citizens, or on their commitment to democracy, appear to be mistaken"[12].

However as highlighted by Franklin many established democracies experienced a large period without elections through World War II and this bore witness to increased socialising and integration of civil life as this increased sharing of ideas and new political attitudes arose.

This is clear in Britain for example, whereby a *Blitz spirit* emerged with a growing community of strangers sharing a common interest and people were increasingly organising events together to raise the spirit and resolve of the wartime population.

The formation of this community and the increased cooperation of the different aspects of society signified a change in political attitudes as at the end of the Second World War the first Social Democratic (Labour Party) was elected into office.

Throughout history changes in contemporary politics have occurred and a prominent example is the Polish solidarity movement which enabled an alternative to communism through the concept and contributed, to some extent, to the collapse the Soviet Union.

The usefulness of Civil Society in terms of

---

[12] Franklin Mark N. *Voter turnout in established democracies since 1945* (Cambridge: Cambridge University Press, 2004), p. 171-199.

TERRY R. LYNCH B.SC. ECON.

understanding change in attitudes concerning contemporary issues in respect to why the states vary in forms of government is plenty, one must dig deeper and find comparative difference in attitudes.

For example, in European states civil society favours state intervention concerning income inequality is more welcomed than in the United States[13] however, most critics would reject this as 'predictable'.

It is evidently hard to measure the beliefs, opinions and emotions of individual citizens towards their form of government; such fundamental values, sentiments and knowledge that give form and substance to political processes[14]) however, Civil Society is useful in measuring these processes.

This is present in the studies of Putnam and figures collected by independent forces. For example, Putnam highlights the essence of Civil Society in itself; however, independent statistical surveys reveal the extent of a particular issue by questioning Civil Society to reveal attitudes.

This is present in the work of Almond and Verba[15] who studied Liberal Democracies and the turbulent issues that have rocked them from 1964 to the present day. The study revealed that attitudes had seen a significant change from that time to the end of the nineties.

These covered: Vietnam and student activism in the 1960s, the oil crisis of the 1970s, the anti-nuclear movement and the rise of ecology groups in the 1980s, privatization and cutbacks to the welfare state in the 1990s.

---

[13] Hague, Rod and Harrop, Martin. *Comparative Government and Politics: An Introduction* (Hampshire: Palgrave, 2001), p.81

[14] Political Culture, in the *Encyclopedia of Democracy* (Congressional Quarterly Books, 1995), p.965.
[15] *Comparative Government and Politics*, Op. cit. p.80

Civil Society, Changing Contemporary Politics with the return of
multi-party politics in the Third World & Religion: An
Introduction

Both in the US and Britain, fine examples of Liberal Democracies, trust in the government has declined. In the UK, trust had fallen from 39 per cent in 1974 to 22 per cent in 1996[16], which would have led to the decline in the Conservative Party and the start of Tony Blair's New Labour reign.

Obviously, as Civil Society was the origin of the survey, it shows how it can lead to a greater understanding of change in contemporary politics. The figures showed a shift away from 'civic' culture and a more removed and remote attitude to politics.

With such declining turnout, (especially in the United States) Almond and Verba concluded that participant culture was discarded, a concept regarded as the principle of democracy.

Basing one's argument on a finite balance of input of participant culture into 'civil' culture[17] it is to remedy that contemporary civil society is indeed leaning away from fundamental elective duties and towards more direct courses of action.

As membership of pressure groups are increasing to demonstrate to government that society is in disagreement with policy and increasingly becoming distant from the political norms.

This shows us that in contemporary politics people are less directly involved in the mechanisms of government and no longer feel obliged to vote for a government which they could have some kind of input.

---

[16] Ibid.
[17] Almond and Vera, Ibid.

2 CIVIL SOCIETY AND RELIGION

We have covered what civil society is in the political context but what about in the religious, how it fits-in and within the natural order, within the fabric of humanity itself. The Pope Benedict XVI teaches that civil society starts with the family. The Pope teaches that "marriage and the family constitute a decisive foundation for the healthy development of civil society, countries and peoples." And, as "the reception and transmission of divine love are realized in the mutual commitment of the spouses, in generous and responsible procreation, in the care and education of children, work and social relationships, with attention to the needy, in participation in church activities, in commitment to civil society". [18]

But does the cell of the family lead to greater commitment to civil society and how does this notion relate to humanity, how does it fit-in? Andrew Copson, citing a government survey looks at the figures in table six and measures the "civic engagement and formal

---

[18] Pope Benedict XVI, "Address to participants at the Plenary Assembly of the Pontifical Council for the Family" (Dec. 1, 2011)

Civil Society, Changing Contemporary Politics with the return of
multi-party politics in the Third World & Religion: An
Introduction

volunteering at least once in the past year" and finds that
the person with no faith is just as active as one of faith. [19]

Copson is saying that it is not the preserve of the
religious to do well within civil society, showing that this is
indeed a shared responsibility. In fact by statistics alone
one may say that religious affiliation makes little difference
to the numbers of volunteers.

The desire to help and serve is engraved on the human
heart and as I said in my previous book *Prayer: teach us to
pray (Luke 11: 1-13)* "*Heart speaks unto heart* and people find
comfort in groups that feel the same longing for truth." [20]

Philanthropy, volunteering, charity are areas which
both humanists and people of faith can share a common
interest, however it is within the realm of faith that truth
and salvation can be found, the notion which is most
puzzling to humanists. Yet as charity is found in truth,
religious charities can and indeed are run by both religious
and non-religious people such as Jeremy Paxman, of the
British Broadcasting Corporation's Newsnight who has no
fixed belief. Paxman is a patron of two major Catholic
charities for the homeless such as the Cardinal Hume
Centre and Anchor House.

As Copson writes "if a person doing good is doing it
because she thinks God wants her to or out of a humanist
sense of obligation to fellow human beings".

The parable of *The Good* Samaritan (Luke 10: 29-37) is

---

[19] http://www.humanism.org.uk/news/view/899 ,
Table   6
http://webarchive.nationalarchives.gov.uk/201209191327
19/www.communities.gov.uk/documents/statistics/xls/1
992761.xls
[20] Lynch, Terry R., "*Prayer: teach us to pray (Luke 11:1-13)*"
(U.S.A., Amazon, 2013) p. 2

to an extent an example of civil society in action that of empathy across boundaries, showing that the religious who are not of the right spirit are actually somewhat ignorant of their civic duties and that of being human. And as such Pope Benedict reveals that we should not forget the origins of charity in truth as Britain must acknowledge its Christian tradition and Christians be part of the national conversation, not removing themselves from the world and instructed in the spirit as Christ says in **John** 17:15.

Knowing that everyone however objectionable their behaviour, or pitiful their demeanour is a child of a loving God should help religious people to turn to secular people in need and as Leviticus 19:18 teaches us must be loved.

Catholic tradition is full of heroes who reach out over the boundaries of social prejudice and disgust, from Peter Claver and St. Damien tending suppurating lepers to Blessed Mother Teresa, whose mission was to bring dignity to the dying whom others recoiled from touching. Humanists, too, can point to many great heroes who were as moved by empathy into acting for others as *heart speaks unto heart*.

With the instructional formation of faith schools and the gift of the Holy Spirit that guides act of charity, religion builds civil society in a way that secular civic participation does not.

Prime Minister David Cameron's big society is an aim at strengthening and maintaining civic society which can sympathise with traditional conservatism (with less government involvement and private enterprise) and this is revealed in Robert Putnam's research that big society (civil society) and charitable civic action is closely linked to organisation and membership.

Networks of participation deepen involvement with others: most people get involved because someone they trust suggests it. While this is as true of religious as non-religious people, it is simply a fact that religion generates networks of participation that are far stronger, more

Civil Society, Changing Contemporary Politics with the return of
multi-party politics in the Third World & Religion: An
Introduction

lasting, and more committed than secular civic
organisations are capable of.

The organisational capacity of the Catholic church in
England and Wales is some 2,300 schools, 3,000 parishes
and the wealth of activity that it generates (19,000
volunteers, 9,000 employees, spending some £170m a year
in the service of approximately 800,000 people) religious
contribution to the civic society cannot be under-
estimated.

Religious communities invest much with the sunk costs
stimulating the capacity for generating participation and
engagement through this *social capital*.

This where civil society and religious social capital is
disproportionately important to the poor, because they
lack other forms of capital – financial and human
(educational) and allows for a more socially responsible
capitalism. That is why logically speaking religious
contribution is especially important among the less well-
off, not just in meeting material needs and wants but, more
significantly, in generating civic and political participation
which in turn builds human and financial capital. This
strengthens the relations between communities and
strengthens civil society.

Civil groups such as London Citizens, Blue Labour and
Red Tories with their organisational structure make this
contribution work effectively; and they make it because the
evidence for it is overwhelming, especially so of the
church.

There are many ways of meeting needs: through
privately-funded charities, secular or religious; through the
state via welfare provision. Strong civil society can relieve
the burden on state obligations and can further welfare
provision at no extra cost to the state and this is why
Cameron's big society can be alluring if more is done to
stimulate and integrate. Most of them require people to

support them, through time and money and with increasing disposable funds in the economy, or to an extent, global economy through strengthened socially responsible capitalism might be religious or non-religious. But social capital that is networks of belonging, trust, and engagement is increased disproportionately by faith institutions which are the primary motors of civil society and strengthened by the family unit which ensures its legacy. What the Putnam research showed is that the rapid shrinking of civil society of most of the 20th century closely correlates to the diminution of religious practice and arguably we have been here before which is why renewal and inheritance through family participation is so important.

In the early 19th century (as today) there was feral individualism, social-Darwinism, unbridled global capitalism, social inequalities, disintegration of the family, violent riots etcetera but within a few generations from the late 19th century, that had been put right.

The revitalisation of civic life in the last decades of the 19th century saw an explosion of forms of civic engagement (not just religious, but ethnic, fraternal, labour, professional, philanthropic, humanist) which over time reduced crime, restored order, and led to profound social reforms. In this revitalisation of civic life the role of faith institutions, alongside that of others, was crucial, and will be again. The defence of marriage in relation to the family is equally important as civil society itself as it is the unit whereby divine love manifests into charitable action in truth with generational instruction through the Spirit.

3 ACCOUNTING FOR THE RETURN OF MULTI-PARTY DEMOCRACY TO THE THIRD WORLD AND CAN DEMOCRATISATION BE SAID TO HAVE IMPROVED THE LIVES OF POOR PEOPLE?

Multi-party democracy (MPD) and capitalism seem to be the most accepted doctrine for the modern emphasis for poverty reduction however to what extent and does democracy really bring any improvements to the lives of poor people?

With the return of MPD to the third world can democracy and globalisation powered by "turbo-capitalism"[21] result in a new global civil society motivated with the aim of civilizing uncivil capitalism now succeed in improving the lives of poor people as democratisation establishes a healthier civil society?

---

[21] Keane, John. *'Global Civil Society?'* (Cambridge: Cambridge University Press, 2003) p65-74.

Huntington (1991) theorises the third "waves of democratisation … in the modern world" came in between 1974-1991 within the third world states of Latin America and parts of Africa, however was revised to the second wave in 1958-1975 in much of Latin America and postcolonial Africa. To account for the return of MPD to the third world we must look at the domestic with the origins of civil movements with the pro-democracy protests and the legalisation of opposition parties in the 1990s following these waves of democratisation.[22]

Antonio Gramsci reveals a "third force"[23] between the state and the market with a realm of potential emancipation to the lives of the poor people. With increased globalisation and reconciliation of the world economy it can be argued as by Andrew Linklater, that a new idealistic world political community has become possible. However, this is a complex issue and globalisation has different experiences within different communities especially so in the third world.

With the triumph of liberal democracy at the end of the cold war referring to Fukuyama, the marginalisation and diffusion of the third world and the shift of strategic importance to Eastern Europe was the return of democracy due to external political pressures for democratisation as aid was offered conditionally upon improved political pluralism?

Does Huntington's argument of a *clash of civilizations*

---

[22] For an example of the demand for MPD and the birth of political pressure groups within civil society in Malawi, read: Wiseman, John A. (ed.) 'Democracy *and Political Change in sub-Saharan Africa*'. (London: Routledge, 1995) p.156-164.

[23] For further argument on how the welfare state, as a third force, can achieve emancipation for the disempowered read: '*Power Resource Management and the welfare state*' (London: University of Toronto Press, 1998) p142.

now have more force as the western policy of democratisation is bringing the third world into a new co-operation within a liberal democratic world order aiding the plight of the poor peoples?

Has Christianity in the third world played a part in the calls for democratisation and poverty reduction through teachings of compassion, due to westernisation or was it purely due to the failings of the authoritarian nature of rule that bought democracy to the third world?[24]

In Kenya the Church played a significant role in supporting the secret ballot and as an advocate of democracy opposed the one-party system following the regimes silencing of politicians and repressive moves towards civil society, however it was also collaboration between professional bodies such as the Law Society of Kenya (LSK) that bought a significant pro-democracy force. However the conditions pinned to aid seemed avoidable for a pro-western regime as Kenya demonstrated that despite concerns over the direction and increased tyranny of President Moi's regime aid agencies, donors and world governments were not going to abandon a 'legitimately elected' ally.[25]

Did internal pressures such as the failings of

---

[24] For further in-depth discussion of religious moves for democratization read: Sigmund, Paul E. *'Christian Democracy, Liberation Theology, and Political Culture in Latin America'* in Diamond, Larry (ed.) *'Political Culture & Democracy in Developing Countries'*. (London: Lynne Rienner, 1994) p211-228.

[25] Throup, David and Hornsby, Charles. *'Multi-Party Politics in Kenya: the Kenyatta & Moi States & the triumph of the system of the system in the 1992 election'* (Oxford: James Currey, 1998) p.55

authoritarian rule, economic decline, and social injustice, the loss of legitimacy for one-party regimes and the pro-democracy movements combined with the external pressures that motivated the return of MPD?

Zambia would suggest that the domestic problems were mainly created by the structural adjustment programmes (SAP) by the international momentary fund (IMF) and World Bank (WB) that created the food crisis in 1990 and resulted in a destabilisation, loss of legitimisation and moves towards democracy.

Capping farming subsidiaries through budget rationalisation these programmes intended to aid economic recovery limit the ability to meet demand therefore little consideration is given to provisions for cushioning the poor against their possible side effects due to the speed of implementation, planning and preparation.

Karl Marx argued that economic development was linked to the mode of production and exchange that shapes the social-political institutions, therefore the SAPs disrupted production and hindered development, certainly capped trade subsidiaries disrupted food production and underdeveloped industry, and debt hampers exchange or trade with the rest of the developed world.

Economic and food security crisis in Zambia increased vocalization of the pro-democracy movement combined with external pressures from donors resulted in President Kenneth Kaunda's legalisation of political parties resulting in greater political pluralism and marking the start of MPD in the 1990s.

However was this multi-party system more to do with factions than legitimate parties and did parties what Almond and Verba called the corner stone of democracy really improve the lives of poor people?

Does this advocate a more state directed economy or a sign that uncivil capitalism does not always work in favour of both partners and that more work needs to be done on the side of global civil society on improving standards and regularisation of the third world economy.

This presents the idea that although democracy improves the participation and rights of the poor within politics and civil society it does not however provide shelter or nourishment.

Following the debt crisis in 1980 the Washington Consensus advocated that the state should not take a more directive role and strengthened capitalist principles of privatisation of state enterprises and reduction of trade barriers, while implemented initially in Latin America[26] has this been taken a step further with the privatisation of security in Africa or is this one example of preventative strategy from years of civil wars and unrest?

Does this privatisation of security reveal the failings of the third world states to provide adequate security for their citizens or is it simply capitalism at its finest, valued at 85 billion dollars with a growth rate of 6-8 percent.[27] It is open to analysis as to whether this revenue has aided the ability of the democratic welfare state to provide for the poorest communities or whether it has hindered improvement to the poor with only rich areas gaining protection.

The third world economy is neo-colonial based on a dependency upon western industrialised nations. Tanzania illustrates an attempt to break from this trend and produce a self-reliant industrial economy that with strong socialist

---

[26] Peeler, John. '*Building democracy in Latin America*' (London: Lynne Rienner, 1998) p141-142.

[27] For further information on the project by Dr. Rita Abrahamsen and Professor Michael Williams, visit: '*The Globalization of Private Security*' with concentration on South Africa, Nigeria, Kenya, and Sierra Leone. Http://users.aber.ac.uk/rbh/privatesecurity/project.html

ideology aims to spread the benefits more evenly both spatially and structurally however there is still reliance upon importing secondary products. There are no actual markets for products that Africa actually produces and there is a pressing need for developing countries to access existing channels of world trade, George Monbiot argues doing so "in direct competition with big business overseas is like learning to swim in a torrent: you will be swept away and drowned long before you acquire the necessary expertise". [28]

Monbiot calls upon the World Trade Organisation (WTO) to create an "infant industry protection" that would allow an internal economy to develop and allow a degree of protectionism to enable these industries to compete with international companies and achieve universal fair trade. Arguing that the rich countries are hindering the transfer of wealth and improvement to the lives of the poor by defending their markets against imports from poor countries, "The policy makes sense. Established industries have capital, experience and economies of scale on their side; infant industries in poor nations do not".[29]

Monbiot argues that the WTO cannot do this as the IMF refuses to allow loans on this pretext. The author of *'a manifesto for a new world order'* he argues that we must embrace capitalism, capture it and shape it to produce a global democratic revolution.

Non-governmental movements such as Fair Trade, whereby third world producers get a fixed sum to cover production costs in all products sold this is now growing into big business with companies such as Nestlé affiliating themselves with the foundation challenging the hold of

---

[28] Monbiot, George. "Universal Fair Trade" Http://www.monbiot.com/archives/2003/09/08/univers al-fair-trade/
[29] Ibid.

exploitive companies who are motivated by profits and exploit the poor communities. However with companies such as Nestlé under boycott by pressure groups is this association more to do with improving their company's image?[30]

Certainly with help of international charities such as the Make Poverty History campaign which has managed to pressure the G8 Nations to scrap third world debt, aid can now reach the poor people rather than pay-off debts however the "promise to the world's poor is being broken". Furthermore the United Nation's (UN) Millennium development goals to tackle extreme poverty, disease, and inequality by 2015 have failed so far according to the 2005 Human Development Report.

Globalisation in theory helps redevelopment of third world economies however they are unregulated by a weak state where workers have little protection by law and therefore exploit local communities and pay relatively low wages in some cases creating more problems.

Within a healthy civil society, non-governmental organisations (NGOs) can aid the development of local poor communities and with foreign or state aid can revitalise the economy.

Democracy, of one person one vote, combined with uncivil capitalism is no guarantee of social and economic equality and justice; however with the emergence of democracy the poor are now empowered and can work within the mechanism of government to gain significant protectorate or welfare legislation within theoretically a healthy economy.

---

[30] For more detailed information on the origin of this boycott, visit: http://www.babymilkaction.org/pages/boycott.html

Nigeria rich in oil reserves, ranking eleventh in Organization of Petroleum Exporting Countries, takes a capitalist line of development which includes privatising state-owned entities with high oil prices the driving force behind Nigeria's economic growth in 2005. The country's gross domestic product (GDP) grew approximately 4.5 percent in 2005 and is expected to grow 6.2 percent in 2006 but with this growth and considerable oil wealth have the lives of the poor of Niger improved? No. It is still ranked one of the poorest countries in the world with 70 percent living in poverty and an income of only 1, 000 dollars per capita. However some 60 percent debt had been cancelled in October 2005 but with conditions and 12.4 billion dollars of arrears. However with an additional 34 percent of debt being scrapped, Nigeria will still owe debts to many leading nations. However the IMF can now monitor development without disbursing loans. [31]

Was the country's transition to democracy due to the failure of previous non-democratic and non-capitalist system to produce the current trend of economic growth following the failure to survive the oil crisis of mid-1970s, which was defined by the UN as "the most seriously affected by the oil crisis" along with 20 other African nations?

Paul Cammack argues that the doctrine of democracy and capitalism for political development has triumphed and now as argued by Fukuyama the world will be concerned with "resolving mundane economic and technical problems"[32] signifying economic development for the third world and thus an emphasis upon poverty and debt reduction following the end of the Cold war.

---

[31] "Energy Information Administration". Http://www.eia.doe.gov/emeu/cabs/Nigeria/Background.html

[32]Huntington, Samuel P. *The Clash of civilizations and the remaking of world order'* (London: The Free Press, 2002) p. 31

Civil Society, Changing Contemporary Politics with the return of multi-party politics in the Third World & Religion: An Introduction

As third world debt, development and the balance of trade is run not by its people but by a handful of unelected or under-elected executives who make the decisions on economic development policy and control its benefits to poor communities prioritising debt repayment.

It would seem that with the spread of democracy throughout the third world and the return of multi-party politics these unelected executives are placed under further pressure from an increasing civil society that through various associations campaigns for economic and through the accountable democratic third world government more accountability. With the new waves of democratic revolution in the third world there are now needs for further reform of the UN for better accountability and increased abilities to achieve set aims for policy reduction, reform of the WTO to enable third world industry to develop and compete with international companies and see the benefits filter through to improving the life's of poor people.

Improvement to the poor through economic development and so political stability can come only if the third world can disengage from its exploitative, dependant relationship with the industrialised nations.

Social-political progress is determined not so much by economic failure or progress but rather the reverse that an economy's success or progress is itself caused by the social and political system to which they operate and that the only effective answer to economic failure is to change the social and political context.

Therefore democracy and capitalism is the most effective answer for improving the lives of the poor but until the third world industry can internally develop to compete with multinational companies through protectionism and debt is scrapped or reduced, the benefits to the poor will not be significant.

BIBLIOGRAPHY

CHAPTER ONE

BOOKS

1. Hague, Rod and Harrop, Martin. *Comparative Government and Politics: An Introduction* (Hampshire: Palgrave, 2001)

2. Heywood, Andrew. *Key Concepts in Politics* (Hampshire: Palgrave, 2000).

3. 4th Ed. Lipset, Seymour Martin. *Encyclopedia of Democracy* (Congressional Quarterly Books, 1995)

4. Linklater, Andrew. *Transformation of political community: ethical foundations of the post-Westphalian era* (Cambridge: Polity Press, 1998).

5. Franklin Mark N. *Voter turnout in established democracies since 1945* (Cambridge: Cambridge University Press, 2004).

Civil Society, Changing Contemporary Politics with the return of
multi-party politics in the Third World & Religion: An
Introduction

6. Edwards, Michael, *Civil society* (Hampshire: Palgrave, 2004).

7. Tester Keith, *Civil society*, (London: Routledge, 1992).

8. Hall, John A. (ed.) *Civil society: theory, history, comparison.* (Cambridge: Polity Press, 1995).

9. Keane, John, *Global civil society?* (Cambridge: Cambridge University Press, 2003).

10. Garrad, John. Democratisation in Britain: Elites, civil society and reform since 1800 (Hampshire: Palgrave, 2002).

11. Trentmann, Frank (ed.) *Paradoxes of civil society: new perspectives on modern German and British history.* (Berghahn Books, 2000).

12. Tocqueville de, Alexis, *Democracy in America.* Frohnen, Bruce (ed.), (Washington DC: Regnery Publishing, 2002).

13. McAfee, Noëlle, *Habermas, Kristeva and citizenship.* (New York: Cornell University Press, 2000).

14. Faulks, Keith. *Citizenship* (London: Routledge, 2000).

15. Marx, Karl. *Selected writings [of] Karl Marx /* (ed.) McLellan, David. (Oxford: Oxford University Press, 1977).

16. Marx, Karl, *Basic writings on politics and philosophy /*

Karl Marx and Freidrich Engels; (ed.) Feuer, Lewis S., (New York: Anchor Books, Doubleday and Company, 1959).

17. Walzer, Michael, *Towards a Global Civil Society.* (Oxford: Berghan Books, 1995).

18. Poggi, Gianfranco. *Images of Society: essays on the sociological theories of Tocqueville, Marx and Durkheim* (London: Oxford University Press, 1972).

19. O'Connor, Julia S., Olsen, Gregg M. *Power Resource Management and the welfare state* (London: University of Toronto Press, 1998)

INTERNET

1. "Civil Society & the UN", http://www.un.org/issues/civilsociety/, (Cited 18/11/2005).

2. Diamond, Larry. *"Civil society and the Development of Democracy".* http://www.march.es/ceacs/publicaciones/working/ archivos/1997_101.pdf, (Cited 19/11/2005).

CHAPTER TWO

BOOKS

1. Lynch, Terry R., *"Prayer: teach us to pray (Luke 11:1-13)" (U.S.A., Amazon, 2013)*

Civil Society, Changing Contemporary Politics with the return of multi-party politics in the Third World & Religion: An Introduction

INTERNET

2. Pope Benedict XVI, "Address to participants at the Plenary Assembly of the Pontifical Council for the Family", http://www.vatican.va/holy_father/benedict_xvi/speeches/2011/december/documents/hf_ben-xvi_spe_20111201_pc-family_en.html (Dec. 1, 2011)

3. British Humanist Association, "New Government statistics illustrate 'madness' of privileged place in policy for religion", http://www.humanism.org.uk/news/view/899 (Sept. 22, 2011)

4. Table 6 http://webarchive.nationalarchives.gov.uk/20120919132719/www.communities.gov.uk/documents/statistics/xls/1992761.xls (Sept. 2011)

CHAPTER THREE

BOOKS

1. Cammack, Paul. *"Capitalism and democracy in the Third World: the doctrine for political development"* (London; Leicester University, 1997)

2. Huntington, Samuel P. *"The Clash of civilizations and the remaking of world order"* (London: The Free Press, 2002)

3. Keane, John. *"Global Civil Society?"* (Cambridge: Cambridge University Press, 2003).

4. Monbiot, George. *"A manifesto for a new world order"* (London: Flamingo, 2003).

5. Peeler, John. *"Building democracy in Latin America"* (London: Lynne Rienner, 1998)

6. Sigmund, Paul E. *"Christian Democracy, Liberation Theology, and Political Culture in Latin America"* in Diamond, Larry (ed.) *"Political Culture & Democracy in Developing Countries"*. (London: Lynne Rienner, 1994)

7. Throup, David and Hornsby, Charles. *"Multi-Party Politics in Kenya: the Kenyatta & Moi States & the triumph of the system of the system in the 1992 election"* (Oxford: James Currey, 1998)

8. Wiseman, John A. (ed.) *"Democracy and Political Change in sub-Saharan Africa"*. (London: Routledge, 1995)

9. *"Power Resource Management and the welfare state"* (London: University of Toronto Press, 1998)

INTERNET

10. Babymilkaction.org http://www.babymilkaction.org/pages/boycott.html (12/03/2006).

11. Dr. Rita Abrahamsen and Professor Michael Williams. *"The Globalization of Private Security"* Http://users.aber.ac.uk/rbh/privatesecurity/project.html (12/03/2006).

12. "Energy Information Administration".

http://www.eia.doe.gov/emeu/cabs/Nigeria/Background.html (12/03/2006).

13. Monbiot, George. "Universal Fair Trade" Http://www.monbiot.com/archives/2003/09/08/universal-fair-trade/ (12/03/2006).

ABOUT THE AUTHOR

Terry Lynch graduated from the University of Wales, Aberystwyth in 2008 with honours as a bachelor of social science and economics from the department of international politics. Studying the course international politics and military history. Terry covered a variety of themes; On War from Carl Von Clausewitz, St. Thomas Aquinas' just war theology, twenty-first century warfare and others.

www.ingramcontent.com/pod-product-compliance
Lightning Source LLC
Chambersburg PA
CBHW070405290526
45790CB00004B/1646